THE EVOLUTION
OF AFRICA'S MAJOR NATIONS

Angola

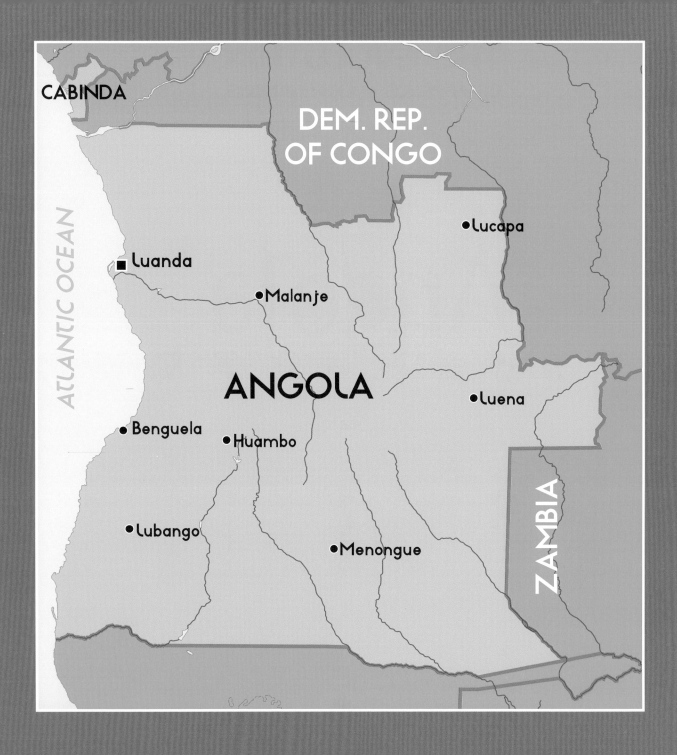

THE EVOLUTION
OF AFRICA'S MAJOR NATIONS

Angola

Rob Staeger

Mason Crest
Philadelphia

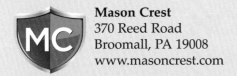

Mason Crest
370 Reed Road
Broomall, PA 19008
www.masoncrest.com

CPSIA Compliance Information: Batch #EAMN2013-4. For further information,
contact Mason Crest at 1-866-MCP-Book.

First printing

1 3 5 7 9 8 6 4 2

Library of Congress Cataloging-in-Publication Data

Staeger, Rob.
  Angola / Rob Staeger.
      p. cm. — (Evolution of Africa's major nations.)
  Includes bibliographical references and index.
  ISBN 978-1-4222-2192-1 (hardcover)
  ISBN 978-1-4222-2220-1 (pbk.)
  ISBN 978-1-4222-9432-1 (ebook)
  1. Angola—Juvenile literature. I. Title. II. Series: Evolution of Africa's major nations.
  DT1269.S73 2012
  967.3—dc22
                          2011018538

Africa: Facts and Figures

The African Union

Algeria

Angola

Botswana

Burundi

Cameroon

Democratic Republic
  of the Congo

Egypt

Ethiopia

Ghana

Ivory Coast

Kenya

Liberia

Libya

Morocco

Mozambique

Nigeria

Rwanda

Senegal

Sierra Leone

South Africa

Sudan

Tanzania

Uganda

Zimbabwe

Table of Contents

Introduction   6
Robert I. Rotberg

Riches in the Land   11

From Colony to Civil War   19

The Government of Angola   35

A Postwar Economy   45

The People of Angola   57

Cities and Communities   69

A Calendar of Angolan Festivals   74

Recipes   76

Glossary   78

Project and Report Ideas   80

Chronology   82

Further Reading/Internet Resources   84

For More Information   85

Index   86

Africa: Progress, Problems, and Promise

Robert I. Rotberg

Africa is the cradle of humankind, but for millennia it was off the familiar, beaten path of global commerce and discovery. Its many peoples therefore developed largely apart from the diffusion of modern knowledge and the spread of technological innovation until the 17th through 19th centuries. With the coming to Africa of the book, the wheel, the hoe, and the modern rifle and cannon, foreigners also brought the vastly destructive transatlantic slave trade, oppression, discrimination, and onerous colonial rule. Emerging from that crucible of European rule, Africans created nationalistic movements and then claimed their numerous national independences in the 1960s. The result is the world's largest continental assembly of new countries.

There are 53 members of the African Union, a regional political grouping, and 48 of those nations lie south of the Sahara. Fifteen of them, including mighty Ethiopia, are landlocked, making international trade and economic growth that much more arduous and expensive. Access to navigable rivers is limited, natural harbors are few, soils are poor and thin, several countries largely consist of miles and miles of sand, and tropical diseases have sapped the strength and productivity of innumerable millions. Being landlocked, having few resources (although countries along Africa's west coast have tapped into deep offshore petroleum and gas reservoirs), and being beset by malaria, tuberculosis, schistosomiasis, AIDS, and many other maladies has kept much of Africa poor for centuries.

Thirty-two of the world's poorest 44 countries are African. Hunger is common. So is rapid deforestation and desertification. Unemployment rates are often over 50 percent, for jobs are few—even in agriculture. Where Africa once

A family plays and does laundry in the shadow of bullet-riddled ruins in Kuito. During the 1990s, this city in central Angola was badly damaged during seiges by rebel forces during the Angolan Civil War.

was a land of small villages and a few large cities, with almost everyone engaged in growing grain or root crops or grazing cattle, camels, sheep, and goats, today more than half of all the more than 1 billion Africans, especially those who live south of the Sahara, reside in towns and cities. Traditional agriculture hardly pays, and a number of countries in Africa—particularly the smaller and more fragile ones—can no longer feed themselves.

There is not one Africa, for the continent is full of contradictions and variety. Of the 750 million people living south of the Sahara, at least 150 million live in Nigeria, 85 million in Ethiopia, 68 million in the Democratic Republic of the Congo, and 49 million in South Africa. By contrast, tiny Djibouti and

The statue of Cristo Rei (Christ the King) is a well-known landmark in Lubango, a city in southwestern Angola.

Equatorial Guinea have fewer than 1 million people each, and prosperous Botswana and Namibia each are under 2.2 million in population. Within some countries, even medium-sized ones like Zambia (12 million), there are a plethora of distinct ethnic groups speaking separate languages. Zambia, typical with its multitude of competing entities, has 70 such peoples, roughly broken down into four language and cultural zones. Three of those languages jostle with English for primacy.

Given the kaleidoscopic quality of African culture and deep-grained poverty, it is no wonder that Africa has developed economically and politically less rapidly than other regions. Since independence from colonial rule, weak governance has also plagued Africa and contributed significantly to the widespread poverty of its peoples. Only Botswana and offshore Mauritius have been governed democratically without interruption since independence. Both are among Africa's wealthiest countries, too, thanks to the steady application of good governance.

Aside from those two nations, and South Africa, Africa has been a continent of coups since 1960, with massive and oil-rich Nigeria suffering incessant periods of harsh, corrupt, autocratic military rule. Nearly every other country on or around the continent, small and large, has been plagued by similar bouts of instability and dictatorial rule. In the 1970s and 1980s Idi Amin ruled Uganda capriciously and Jean-Bedel Bokassa proclaimed himself emperor of the Central African Republic. Macias Nguema of Equatorial Guinea was another in that same mold. More recently Daniel arap Moi held Kenya in thrall and Robert Mugabe has imposed himself on once-prosperous Zimbabwe. In both of those cases, as in the case of Gnassingbe Eyadema in Togo and the late Mobutu Sese Seko in Congo, these presidents stole wildly and drove entire peoples and their nations into penury. Corruption is common in Africa, and so are a weak rule-of-law framework, misplaced development, high expenditures on soldiers and low expenditures on health and education, and a widespread (but not universal) refusal on the part of leaders to work well for their followers and citizens.

Conflict between groups within countries has also been common in Africa. More than 12 million Africans have been killed in civil wars since 1990, while another 9 million have become refugees. Decades of conflict in Sudan led to a January 2011 referendum in which the people of southern Sudan voted overwhelmingly to secede and form a new state. In early 2011, anti-government protests spread throughout North Africa, ultimately toppling long-standing regimes in Tunisia and Egypt. That same year, there were serious ongoing hostilities within Chad, Ivory Coast, Libya, the Niger Delta region of Nigeria, and Somalia.

Despite such dangers, despotism, and decay, Africa is improving. Botswana and Mauritius, now joined by South Africa, Senegal, Kenya, and Ghana, are beacons of democratic growth and enlightened rule. Uganda and Senegal are taking the lead in combating and reducing the spread of AIDS, and others are following. There are serious signs of the kinds of progressive economic policy changes that might lead to prosperity for more of Africa's peoples. The trajectory in Africa is positive.

Angola is home to a variety of geographical features. (Opposite) Epupa Falls is located near the border with Namibia. The spectacular waterfall on the Cunene River drops 120 feet (37 meters). (Right) Cloud-covered view of the Serra da Leba mountain range, which is located in the south of Angola near Lubango.

Riches in the Land

ANGOLA IS LOCATED in Central Africa, one of the most resource-rich areas in the world. Off the coast of Angola are deep reserves of oil, while diamonds can be found in the northeastern part of the country. However, despite these natural assets Angola's people are among the world's poorest. A long-running civil war for control of Angola's resources has had a devastating effect on the country's citizens and economy.

GEOGRAPHY

The Republic of Angola is located on the west coast of Africa, north of Namibia. To the east lie Zambia and the Democratic Republic of the Congo (formerly Zaire). To the west, Angola has 994 miles (1,600 kilometers) of Atlantic Ocean coastline.

Angola's northern border is formed by the Congo River. However, more Angolan territory lies beyond the river. The *exclave* of Cabinda is part of Angola, but is separated from the rest of the country by a strip of land controlled by the Democratic Republic of the Congo (DRC). To Cabinda's north is another country, the Republic of Congo.

Geographically, Angola can be divided into three main regions. To the west, Angola's coastal plains can be as narrow as 15 miles (24 km) in the southern part of the country. The plains grow wider toward the north, reaching almost 100 miles (161 km) across near Angola's capital, Luanda. A series of hills and cliffs divide the coastal region from the interior. In the north, the hills are gradual, but in the south, the cliffs are steep and include the Serra da Chela mountain range. Farther inland the cliffs rise to the plateau region, or *planalto*, which comprises most of Angola's land. Most Angolans live in the *planalto*.

Angola has many rivers, but only two, the Cuanza River in central Angola and the Congo River to the north, are navigable by large boats. Angolans use small boats to travel on other rivers, many of which flow west toward the Atlantic Ocean. One of the largest rivers in southern Angola is the Cubango River. This river forms part of the border between Angola and Namibia, eventually flowing into the Okavango River, the largest waterway in southern Africa. Another major river in southern Angola is the Cunene River, which flows about 700 miles (1,126 km) from the Angolan highlands into Namibia, eventually reaching the Atlantic coast. Many of the Cunene's tributaries only contain water during the rainy season.

THE GEOGRAPHY OF ANGOLA

Location: The west coast of southern Africa, between Namibia and the Democratic Republic of the Congo

Area: Slightly less than twice the size of Texas

total: 481,354 square miles (1,246,700 sq km)

land: 481,354 square miles (1,246,700 sq km)

water: 0 square miles (0 sq km)

Borders: Democratic Republic of the Congo, 1,560 miles (2,511 km), 140 miles (225 km) is the border of the exclave Cabinda Province; Republic of the Congo, 125 miles (201 km); Namibia, 855 miles (1,376 km); Zambia 690 miles (1,110 km); 994 miles (1,600 km) of coastline on Atlantic Ocean.

Climate: Semiarid in south and along coast to Luanda; north has cool, dry season (May to October) and hot, rainy season (November to April)

Terrain: Narrow coastal plain rises abruptly to vast interior plateau

Elevation extremes:

lowest point: Atlantic Ocean, 0 feet (0 m)

highest point: Morro de Moco 8,596 feet (2,620 m)

Natural hazards: flooding on the plateau, caused by local heavy rainfall

Source: CIA World Factbook, 2011.

CLIMATE

All of Angola has distinct dry and rainy seasons, but geography determines how long each season lasts. The southern part of the country has a semi-arid climate. Here the warm rainy season is fairly short, with most precipitation falling from November through February. In the northern areas, which have a wetter tropical climate, it typically rains from September through April, although sometimes the rain eases up in January and February.

Moringa ovalifolia trees, sometimes called "ghost trees," can be found in southwestern Angola. The leaves and fruit of these trees can be eaten by people and livestock.

There is always greater rainfall in the interior of the country than in the coastal areas. This is a side effect of the Atlantic Ocean's cold Benguela Current, which flows north along Angola's coast. Coastal cities like Namibe and Luanda only see an average of two to 13 inches (five to 34 centimeters) of rain, while an inland city like Huambo in the mountain region sees between 31 and 63 inches (80 to 160 cm). Angola's mountains shield the *planalto* from the Benguela Current's drying effect, so the rest of the country receives greater rainfall.

While the heavy rains make it possible to farm in many areas of the country, they also cause dangerous flooding. In 2009, massive flooding in the southern province of Cunene left nearly 25,000 Angolans homeless and, according to Red Cross estimates, affected the health and livelihood of almost 100,000 more.

Temperatures in Angola rise the closer one gets to the equator. In the south, the average year-round temperature in the city of Huambo is 60° Fahrenheit (15.5° Celsius), while farther north, in Cabinda, the average temperature rises to 84.2°F (29°C) in January and 77°F (25.2°C) in July. Because Angola is in the Southern Hemisphere its seasons are opposite of those in the United States, making the dry winter months of July and August the coolest. Snow is very unusual in Angola, but frost occasionally occurs at higher elevations.

VALUABLE TERRAIN

Land is one of Angola's greatest natural assets. The country has between 12 and 20 million acres (4,856,228 to 8,093,713 hectares) of land that is *arable*, or suitable for farming, and the climate and terrain are diverse enough to support a variety of crops. Western Angola, particularly the Uige and Kwanza Sul provinces, have high altitudes and land that is well suited for growing coffee. Sugar cane flourishes in some parts of Angola's northern coast. Farther south the arid coastal areas are ideal for livestock ranches.

However, much Angolan farmland is not cultivated because of the civil war that tore the country apart between 1975 and 2002. Land mines still rid-

The Cunene River is one of Angola's major waterways.

dle the countryside, making many farm fields unusable. During the war many roads were destroyed, making it harder to transport agricultural products to markets. This made farming less profitable. Finally, many people who fled their farms during the conflict are only now returning.

Angola's land is also valuable for the mineral wealth that is found beneath it. The country has massive oil reserves, estimated at nearly 20 billion barrels of oil. Most of the oil is located off the coast of the Cabinda province.

The Lunda Norte and Lunda Sul provinces in the northeast have riches of their own—diamonds. There are two types of diamond deposits in Angola: **alluvial** and **kimberlite**. Alluvial deposits are diamonds found in riverbeds. They have been washed there over the centuries by water and erosion. Angola's alluvial deposits contain an estimated 130 million carats of diamonds. Kimberlite is a type of diamond-rich volcanic rock that occurs in vertical formations known as "pipes." These can be reached only by mining. Angola's kimberlite pipes are estimated to contain 180 million carats.

ECOLOGICAL ISSUES

Angola's decades-long civil war affected every aspect of the country, including the environment. Since the end of the war, Angola's government has focused on rebuilding the economy. Oil production has expanded, and new diamond mines were opened in 2007. Unfortunately the government has paid little attention to the country's ecological problems, so economic growth comes at a high price. Communities have cut down forests faster than new trees can grow, which will cause problems in the future. Not only will indigenous species lose their habitat, but also the topsoil will erode without plant life to hold the dirt

Angola's giant sable antelopes are in danger of becoming extinct. The animals can be found roaming the Luanda game preserve.

in place. Widespread erosion could severely damage any farming prospects.

Angola does have 10 conservation areas and national parks, but these have also been hit hard by the civil war. In most places, it is unknown what the long-term effects are on the species that inhabited the parks. Some may have been wiped out completely. The numbers of rhinos, elephants, and buffalo left in Angola are unknown, as many have migrated to safer areas.

One species native to Angola that is in danger is the Angolan giant sable, a type of antelope. Unlike other antelopes, the giant sable's horns rise vertically from its head before curving backward.

In Quicama National Park there have also been sightings of waterbuck, roan antelope, bushbuck, and dwarf forest buffalo. Sea creatures such as manatees, marine turtles, and tarpon have also been spotted off the coast. Bird life was not as affected by the war, although the ongoing deforestation problem may take its toll.

Conflict has dominated Angola's modern history. (Opposite) Angolans celebrate independence from Portugal in November 1975; the banner pictures Jonas Savimbi, leader of a party seeking control of Angola's government. (Right) A selection of land mines on display in Luanda, Angola. Despite efforts to remove these dangerous devices, thousands remain hidden.

2 From Colony to Civil War

THE EARLIEST KNOWN INHABITANTS of the area today known as Angola were the ancestors of today's San people. These people, sometimes known as Bushmen, were hunter-gatherers who migrated seasonally following the animal herds they hunted. These people spoke a language known as Khoisan, which is distinguished by its clicking sounds used as consonants.

Around A.D. 1300 a new group of Bantu-speaking people, known as the Bakongo, arrived from the north. The Bakongo were farmers, so they were able to settle in one place instead of constantly roaming. Some anthropologists believe the Bakongo forced the Bushmen to southern Angola, where pockets of Khoisan speakers can still be found today. Others think that the original inhabitants of Angola were absorbed into Bakongo society.

This detail from a Portuguese monument shows explorers marking their claim to African territory with a stone cross, called a *padrão*.

The Bakongo formed strong societies, such as the Kongo kingdom in the north of Angola. This highly developed African empire controlled an extensive trade network. There were also several smaller kingdoms in the region, most of which promised allegiance to Kongo. One of these was Ndongo, located in what today is northern Angola. Like the Bakongo, the Mbundu people of Ndongo spoke a Bantu language.

Europeans arrived in the region during the 15th century. Beginning in the 1420s, Portuguese rulers began sending out expeditions to map the Atlantic coast of Africa. They hoped to find a sea route around the continent that would allow Portugal easy access to the wealthy markets of Asia. In 1483 a Portuguese explorer named Diogo Cão arrived in present-day Angola, marking his landing spot with a stone pillar. The Portuguese called the region "Angola," which is derived from an African word for king, *ngola*.

Portugal soon established trade arrangements with the Kongo and other African tribes in the region, enabling European traders to exchange weapons and finished goods like cloth and wine for gold, ivory, and most importantly, slaves.

THE SLAVE TRADE

Europeans did not introduce the idea of slavery to Africa—the Kongo and other African kingdoms had always possessed slaves, and they participated willingly in the slave trade with the Portuguese. Slaves became a convenient source of inexpensive labor for Portugal's colony in Brazil. Exploiting the natural resources of Brazil—from gold and silver mines to sugar plantations—made Portugal one of the wealthiest countries in Europe.

Trading agents called *pombieros* acquired slaves from local chiefs who had captured members of other tribes. The *pombiero* then led the slaves—usually several hundred at a time—to the coast in chains. The malnourished, weak slaves who survived this long journey were then rested and fed until they were strong enough to make the grueling voyage across the Atlantic. During the ocean crossing, slaves would spend nearly two months in overcrowded and unsanitary cargo holds. Many Africans died on the way. Over four centuries, it is estimated

Millions of Africans perished during the Atlantic crossing because of the crowded and unsanitary conditions aboard slave ships. Most of the Africans sold as slaves from Angola ended up working in Brazil or on Caribbean plantations.

that about 4 million Angolans were sold into slavery, but only about half of them survived the Atlantic crossing. Nearly all of the Angolan slaves were sent to South America (primarily Brazil) or to colonies in the Caribbean.

Recognizing the value of Angola, the Portuguese began to administer it as a colony, using military force to subdue African tribes that resisted, and sending raiding parties to take slaves. The Kongo and Ndongo sometimes worked with the Portuguese, but at other times they waged wars against the Europeans and against each other.

In 1641 Portuguese commerce in Angola came to a standstill when Dutch soldiers captured several key towns in the colony. The Dutch wanted to take control of the African slave trade, and had already captured Portuguese territories in West Africa and Brazil. The Dutch allied themselves with the Kongo and Matamba and captured the coastal towns of Luanda and Benguela. The colonial government in Angola was forced to move inland to Massangano, and the Dutch began diverting slave shipments to their own colonies.

The loss of Brazil, and of revenue from the slave trade, dealt a heavy blow to Portugal's economy. Portuguese troops counterattacked, and in 1648 the Dutch surrendered Luanda back to Portugal. By 1654, Portugal had regained control of Brazil as well.

Once the Portuguese were back in power, they focused on subduing the rebellious African tribes that had sided with Holland. In 1665 a Portuguese army defeated the Kongo forces. Although the kingdom remained independent, from this point on Kongo's rulers mostly did what the Portuguese told them to do. The same fate befell the Ndongo kingdom in 1671.

In 1836 Portuguese leaders in Angola officially abolished the slave trade. (Colonists would be permitted to own slaves until the 1870s.) However, the government did not have enough ships to enforce this decree, and it had to ask its ally, Great Britain, for help. The British navy helped the Portuguese capture slave ships and arrest their crews.

COLONIAL EXPANSION

Although Portugal ruled the region, there were relatively few Portuguese settlers in Angola. In 1777, for example, there were only 1,600 Europeans living in Angola, and about 90 percent of them were men. Many of the settlers were exiled criminals (known as *degredados*), or Portuguese peasants who could not afford to move to Brazil. With few European women living in the colony, the settlers often married African women. Their mixed-race children became known as *mestiços*. By 1900, there were still fewer than 10,000 people of European descent living in Angola.

During the 19th century, European powers like Britain, France, Germany, and Belgium were exploring and claiming territory in the interior of Africa. In response, Portugal began making a greater effort to expand its Angolan colony farther from the coast. To pay for troops and supplies, the Portuguese rulers of the colony imposed a "hut tax" on the people of Angola. Portugal claimed the area of the Kongo kingdom as part of Angola, and in 1883 occupied Cabinda on the north side of the Congo River.

In 1884 representatives of the European countries that ruled colonies in Africa gathered in Berlin to discuss the future of the continent. At the Berlin Conference, the Europeans formally established the borders of their colonies.

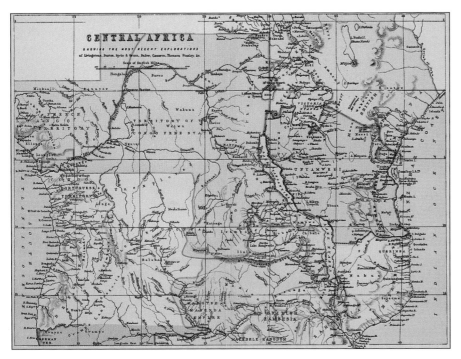

This 19th-century map of Central Africa shows how the European powers carved up the continent into colonies that they could control and exploit. The Portuguese colonies Angola (on the lower Atlantic coast, left) and Mozambique (on the Indian Ocean, lower right) are shaded in light yellow on this map.

Many of these borders, including Angola's, remain essentially the same today. Portugal was denied control of the north bank of the Congo River, stranding Cabinda as an exclave.

The treaty also specified that European countries had to occupy and control the territories they claimed. This meant the Portuguese needed to forcefully subdue the tribes in the interior that were still operating outside of their control. Over the next 25 years, Portugal waged a series of wars against various African tribes in the interior. By 1917, with Portugal's successful conquest of the Dembos of northern Angola, the Portuguese had gained control over the entire country.

ANTI-COLONIALISM

During the 1920s, political turmoil in Portugal had a great impact on Angola. The Portuguese army overthrew the government in a May 1926 coup d'etat, and in 1932, a man named Antonio Salazar came to power as prime minister. Salazar had the powers of a dictator, and he brought a new era to Portugal and its colonies. Salazar's policies promoted Portuguese accomplishments and Catholic values. Rebellious voices were suppressed by his secret police.

As part of his "New State" policy, Salazar wanted to make Angola a more essential part of Portugal. He renamed Angolan towns after Portuguese heroes and replaced the Angolan currency, the angolar, with the Portuguese escudo. Laws were passed limiting how high a *mestiço* or **assimilado** (a native Angolan who had adopted Portuguese customs) could rise in a government job. The law also set different pay scales for the two groups. The qualifications to be considered *assimilado* were strict. In 1950 only 31,000 of the 4 million African Angolans met the requirements. Africans who did not adopt Portuguese ways were categorized as **indigenas** under the new laws, and had even fewer rights than *mestiços* or *assimilados*.

The discriminatory laws changed the tenor of race relations in the colony. Previously, *mestiços* had identified with the Europeans. But once they faced the same discrimination as native Africans, they began to side with them against the Portuguese government. Particularly after the end of World War II in 1945, racial tensions and class strife began to strain the ties between Angola and Portugal.

Agostinho Neto (1922–1979) was one of the founders of the Popular Movement for the Liberation of Angola (in Portuguese, Movimento Popular de Libertação de Angola, or MPLA). This communist organization, which was supported by the Soviet Union and Cuba, emerged as the ruling party when the Portuguese withdrew in 1975. Neto became the country's first president, serving until his death in 1979.

In 1952, 500 Angolan Africans petitioned the United Nations to force Portugal to grant independence to Angola. Nationalist organizations soon began agitating for the end of foreign rule. These groups were generally organized along ethnic and regional lines. The Popular Movement for the Liberation of Angola (MPLA) formed in 1956, when a number of smaller anti-colonial groups joined forces. Led by Agostinho Neto, a doctor and a popular poet, the MPLA's core membership was the upper class in Luanda and other cities, generally of Mbundu ethnic background. MPLA leaders adopted a *communist* ideology and gained support from the Soviet Union.

The MPLA's chief rival was the National Front for the Liberation of Angola (FNLA) led by Holden Roberto. Unlike the MPLA, the FNLA had a rural base. The United States began funding Roberto's group in order to counter the communist influence in the MPLA.

WAR FOR INDEPENDENCE

During the early 1960s, the agitation led to violence. The Portuguese government had been jailing people for anti-colonial activity, and in 1961 the MPLA attacked police stations to free political prisoners. In northwestern Angola, rural Bakongo people raided farms and towns, killing hundreds of European settlers and many African workers as well. Many of the wealthier white settlers left the country; those who remained attacked the Africans in reprisal. Soon the north was engulfed in a race war, which took the Portuguese army six months to stop. More than 40,000 people were killed in the fighting, and many Africans fled as refugees to Zaire.

To ease the unrest, the Salazar government relaxed some of its most discriminatory laws. Salazar also encouraged Portuguese settlers to move to Angola. Although he offered incentives like inexpensive farmland, the plan backfired. Many of the new settlers proved to be incompetent farmers. They soon left for the cities, where they competed with *mestiços* and *assimilados* for jobs. This further increased the racial and political unrest.

In 1966 a group broke off from the FNLA. Led by Jonas Savimbi, the National Union for the Total Independence of Angola (UNITA) was centered in the provinces of Huambo and Bie. UNITA didn't have the resources of the other groups, but it had strong support among the Ovimbundu.

Throughout the next decade, the three groups fought for Angolan independence. Salazar died in 1968, but his successor, Marcello Caetano, continued the New State policies. The government wouldn't budge, even as more and more Portuguese soldiers died in skirmishes.

By 1974 Portugal had lost around 9,000 soldiers in Angola, and 11,000 in Africa overall. Military leaders were tired of fighting a war they could not win and frustrated with the government. On April 25, 1974, Portuguese general Antonio de Spinola led a military coup against Caetano. The uprising became known as the Carnation Revolution because Portuguese citizens showed their support by giving the soldiers red carnations. The revolution was a success. Within two months, the new government of Portugal had granted independence to its African colonies. Angola was free at last.

INDEPENDENCE AND WAR

In January 1975, the leaders of the three competing nationalist factions—Holden Roberto of the FNLA, Agostinho Neto of the MPLA, and Jonas Savimbi of UNITA—met in Luanda to form an interim government for Angola. Elections were scheduled for November 1975.

Their cooperation barely lasted a month. None of the groups trusted the others, and by February 1975 they were fighting in the streets of Luanda. The situation was made worse when foreign countries intervened. The neighboring country of Zaire (now Democratic Republic of the Congo) sent troops to help the FNLA. The Soviet Union and Cuba sent weapons and military advisors to the MPLA, while South Africa supported UNITA. As the fighting heated up, 300,000 Portuguese fled the country.

By November, it was clear there would be no free elections in Angola. The MPLA had crushed FNLA and forced UNITA out of the most populated areas of the country. Thanks to Soviet and Cuban assistance, the MPLA controlled the most crucial parts of Angola: Luanda and the ports of Lobito,

Benguela, and Mocamedes (Namibe). It also controlled Cabinda and its valuable offshore oil fields.

On November 11, 1975, MPLA leader Agostinho Neto declared his country's independence from Portugal as the People's Republic of Angola. Neto established a communist government similar to those in Cuba and the Soviet Union. Under this system the Angolan government controlled businesses and factories, and the MPLA was the only permitted political party.

The civil war did not end, however, as Jonas Savimbi reorganized the defeated supporters of UNITA and FNLA into a resistance movement based in the highlands of Angola. Savimbi continued to receive aid from South Africa, and he also gained financial and military support from the United States, which wanted to counter Soviet influence.

At the time, both the U.S. and the USSR were involved in an undeclared conflict known as the *Cold War.* Rather than fighting directly, each of the world's two superpowers tried to check the worldwide influence of the other by supporting different sides in conflicts around the globe. It was against U.S. foreign policy to allow Angola to become communist without a fight. Otherwise, American leaders feared, neighboring countries might turn to the Soviet Union and establish communist governments as well.

Neto died in 1979 and was succeeded by José Eduardo dos Santos, who maintained the communist MPLA policies. The civil war continued throughout the 1980s, with both the United States and Soviet Union increasing the military aid they sent to their factions in Angola. Some 300,000 Angolans were killed during the first 16 years of fighting.

In 1987–88, a major battle was fought around the city of Cuito Cuanavale involving Cuban and South African troops as well as soldiers from UNITA and the MPLA. The outcome of the battle was inconclusive, as both sides declared victory. Soon after, however, both South Africa and Cuba agreed to withdraw their troops from Angola.

During the late 1980s the Cold War began winding to a close because the Soviet Union was facing serious internal problems. The Soviets began withdrawing their support for Angola and other communist countries. In response, the United States cut its funding for the UNITA rebels. As international financing for the war disappeared, Portuguese leaders stepped in and negotiated a peace treaty. Savimbi and dos Santos signed the agreement, known as the Bicesse Accords, on May 31, 1991, in Lisbon. The treaty included plans to demobilize both armies and hold a national election for a new government in 1992 under the supervision of the United Nations.

THE 1992 ELECTION

The United Nations sent representatives to monitor the peace process and the new elections. The mission was underfunded and undermanned: there were only 800 election monitors to observe 5,820 polling stations throughout the country. Disarming UNITA and the MPLA also went slowly. There were not enough men in the country's new national army, the Angolan Armed Forces (FAA), to carry out the demobilization plan.

The election presented the Angolan people with a difficult choice. José dos Santos's MPLA government was corrupt. Wealth was concentrated in the hands of party leaders and their cronies. This small ruling elite got the best of everything, while most of Angola's people were left with few resources.

However, the alternative candidate, Savimbi, was a ruthless warlord who had allowed his men to commit atrocities during the civil war and had ordered the execution of his political opponents and their families. As the election neared, Savimbi declared that if he lost it would prove that the vote had been rigged.

The final results showed dos Santos getting 49 percent of the vote, while Savimbi got 40 percent. Election observers from the United Nations called the elections "generally free and fair," reporting that there was "no evidence of major, systematic, or widespread fraud." However, Savimbi claimed the vote had been rigged and ordered UNITA supporters to leave the FAA and resume the war against the government.

During this phase of the fighting, the MPLA held the cities and the oil fields, while UNITA took control of the rural interi-

A voter casts her ballot during the presidential election in Luanda, September 1992. When Savimbi lost in the first round of the election, UNITA withdrew from the U.N.-sponsored peace process and restarted the conflict.

International observers watch as representatives of UNITA and the Angolan government sign an agreement to end fighting, known as the Lusaka Protocol.

or and the diamond mines in the northwest.

Each used profits from these resources to fund their military activities. In October 1992, Savimbi launched an assault on Luanda. The battle lasted for three days, but dos Santos's forces repelled the UNITA troops. Then the MPLA began a series of counterattacks intended to exterminate the rebel forces. Eventually, the MPLA recaptured Huambo, UNITA's base of operations.

On November 20, 1994, Savimbi agreed to a new peace deal, ending an outbreak of war that had cost another 200,000 people their lives. The peace deal was called the Lusaka Protocol. Under its terms, Savimbi would become vice president of a new national unity government, which would also include ministers from UNITA. The United Nations sent 7,000 troops to keep the peace while the government was organized. Once the national unity government was established in April 1997, the UN reduced its peacekeeping force to 1,500 soldiers.

In late 1998 the civil war flared up again because of disagreements between UNITA and MPLA leaders. UN peacekeeping troops withdrew in 1999, and the MPLA government used brutal tactics in an effort to wipe out UNITA resistance, destroying cities and villages where Savimbi's supporters sought shelter. In three years, it is estimated that more than 100,000 Angolans were killed, while about 4 million were forced to flee from their devastated homes as refugees.

In February 2002 Savimbi was trapped and killed near the border with Zambia. With his death, many people hoped peace was finally possible. Six weeks later, new UNITA leaders signed a peace agreement called the Luena Understanding. So far, the peace has lasted, and Angolans are working to rebuild their country's roads, hospitals, schools, and other infrastructure devastated during the long civil war.

In 2008, Angola held its first parliamentary elections in 16 years and the MPLA won 191 out of 220 seats in the National Assembly. In January 2010, the National Assembly ratified a new constitution that ushered in several significant changes to both the elections process and the structure of Angola's government.

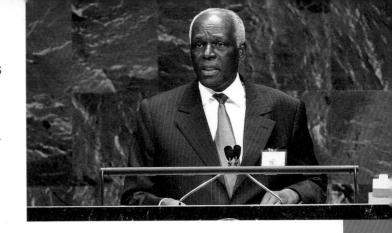

(Opposite) Angolan ministers discuss issues with representatives of Brazil's government during a meeting in Luanda. (Right) Jose Eduardo dos Santos has been president of Angola since 1979. Recent changes to the constitution could allow dos Santos to remain in power until 2022.

3 The Government of Angola

ANGOLA IS A REPUBLIC, a form of government in which political power is in the hands of elected representatives of the citizens. The rules of the government were initially laid down in Angola's first post-colonial constitution, ratified in November 1975. Revisions in 1976 and 1980 reflected the MPLA's socialist agenda and established a one-party state. Further revisions in 1992 officially ended the one-party state, but rival parties have yet to gain a significant foothold in government.

In 2010, a brand new constitution was drafted by a special committee and ratified by the National Assembly, both of which were controlled by a large majority of MPLA representatives. As a result, the new constitution contains many changes that work in their favor.

For example, instead of a general election, Angola's president will now be named by whichever party holds a majority of the seats in the National Assembly. The president, in turn, appoints his own vice president. Future presidents will be limited to two five-year terms, but this rule does not apply to the 30 years for which dos Santos has already held office. It does not go into effect until the next parliamentary elections, which are scheduled for 2012. In theory, this would allow dos Santos to maintain power until 2022.

In another reflection of the MPLA's socialist roots, the new constitution states that all land is officially owned by the government, and only the government can decide who gets to use it. Usage rights will only be granted to Angolan citizens or businesses registered in Angola.

That being said, the new constitution does continue to guarantee individual freedoms, such as freedom of speech and assembly, and prohibits discrimination based on color, race, ethnicity, sex, religion, place of birth, level of education, wealth, or social status.

Angola consists of 18 provinces, which are subdivided into 161 smaller districts. These in turn are broken down even further into quarters (also called communes). Quarters are made up of villages, and larger villages are made up of neighborhoods. Officials in neighborhoods and villages are elected directly by the people. The president appoints leaders at the provincial, district, and commune levels.

As in the United States, Angola's national government is divided into three branches: the legislative, which makes the laws; the executive, which directs national policies and makes sure the laws are carried out; and the judicial, which interprets the laws and dispenses justice. However, unlike in the United States, where the three branches of government are able to balance each other, in Angola the executive branch—and particularly the president—wields most of the government's power.

THE EXECUTIVE BRANCH

The head of the executive branch is the president. José Eduardo dos Santos has held this post since September 21, 1979. The president directs Angola's domestic and international policies, and approves the laws passed by the

Angola's vice president is second only to the president in terms of political power. Here, Vice President Fernando da Piedade Dias dos Santos (left) meets with Portuguese President Anibal Cavaco Silva in Lisbon.

National Assembly. He is also the leader of the military, and has the authority to declare war or make peace.

To help run the government, the president appoints a vice president (formerly a Prime Minister). Fernando da Piedade Dias dos Santos, who had served as prime minister since 2002, was made Angola's first vice president in February 2010. The vice president represents the executive branch in the National Assembly and is in charge of coordinating the activities of Angola's various ministries, which each represent an aspect of the government (such as agriculture, defense, mining, or education). Although some of the ministers report directly to the vice president, others report to "superministers" who coordinate activities between related departments. For example, a superminister manages Angola's "productive sphere," which includes the ministries of agriculture, industry, petroleum and energy, fisheries, transportation and communications, and construction. The "economic and social sphere" includes the ministries of planning, finance, trade, labor and social security, health, and education. Superministers report directly to the prime minister. The heads of each government department form an advisory Council of Ministers that meets regularly with the president and vice president to discuss national issues and government policies.

The constitution specifies that the president can only serve two five-year terms. However, dos Santos's term has been considerably longer. He was not popularly elected when he first took the position in 1979. In 1992 he won the election by default. Although dos Santos received the most votes, he did not get a majority (over 50 percent), so there should have been a runoff election between the top two candidates (in this case, dos Santos and Savimbi). Because Savimbi reignited the civil war immediately after the election, the runoff vote was never held. During the civil war, national elections were continually postponed while the government dealt with the crisis.

In December 2004, dos Santos promised that elections for president and for members of the National Assembly would be held in September 2006. However, in 2006 his government changed the timetable for the elections to 2007. In December 2006 these elections were rescheduled again, with the legislative election planned for the spring or summer of 2008, and a presidential election for 2009. Government officials justified the delays by saying that the additional time was needed to register voters. Opposition parties, including UNITA, were critical of the delays, claiming that dos Santos was using them to remain in power illegally. "If you take into account that the civil war ended in 2002, the president will have been exercising power without legitimacy for seven years" by 2009, complained UNITA spokesman Adalberto Costa.

With the recent ratification of the new constitution, elections were again delayed and dos Santos's term was extended for at least three more years. Elections for seats in the National Assembly are now scheduled for 2012. Whichever party holds a majority will decide who will become Angola's next president.

THE LEGISLATIVE BRANCH

The legislative body of Angola is called the National Assembly. The National Assembly writes the laws for the country. It also writes the national budget and approves international treaties. Unlike the United States Congress, the

Angola's foreign minister, João Bernardo de Miranda (left), meets with United Nations Secretary-General Ban Ki-moon, 2008. Angola has been a member of this international organization of states since 1976.

National Assembly is *unicameral*, meaning it consists of only one assembly of lawmakers.

The National Assembly has 220 members. Each of Angola's 18 provinces elects five members to the National Assembly. The remaining 130 members are elected nationally. In addition, three nonvoting members are appointed to represent the interests of Angolans living in other countries. Two represent Angolans in other African countries; the third represents Angolans living elsewhere in the world. Legislators are supposed to serve a four-year term, but the previous Assembly lasted 16 years.

There is a bridge between the legislative and executive branches of the government called the Council of the Republic. This council is chaired by the president and includes the leaders of the National Assembly, the Supreme Court, and the various political parties represented in the assembly, as well as the Attorney General, the former president, and ten citizens appointed by the president. This group is meant to advise the president on political and administrative matters.

THE JUDICIAL BRANCH

The purpose of the judicial branch is to interpret Angola's laws. The legal system in Angola is based on the Portuguese civil law system, a holdover from the colonial era. The 1992 constitutional changes included some changes to the law as well. These reflected the move from a purely communist system to one based on free markets, as well as the new rights given to political parties.

The highest level of Angola's judicial system is the Supreme Court, or Tribunal da Relação. The Supreme Court rules on matters of national security and also reviews decisions made by lower courts to determine whether they should be upheld or overturned. The president appoints judges to the Supreme Court.

The court system that most people encounter is the people's court system. Established in the late 1970s, these courts handle criminal trials and labor disputes in provincial capitals and other large towns. The government appoints three magistrates for each court. One is a professional judge. The other two are called lay magistrates; they are educated and have undergone several weeks of judicial training, but they are not professional judges. There are no juries, but the judges may consult with members of the community before reaching a decision.

As with many government services in Angola, the judicial system does not have the resources to accommodate the needs of the entire nation. Judges are usually only found in large towns and are not immediately accessible to the public. In addition, although the constitution stipulates that judges should be independent from party politics, the president has occasionally intervened with the Supreme Court to swing important decisions in his party's favor.

POLITICAL PARTIES IN ANGOLA

Several dozen political parties participated in Angola's first multiparty election, held in 1992. However, the country has two major parties, MPLA and UNITA, which received most of the votes and thus control most of the seats in the National Assembly.

The current ruling party, MPLA, is organized into three bodies: the Political Bureau, the Central Committee, and the Party Congress. The president chairs each of these bodies. The largest of these groups is the Party Congress. Included in the Congress are representatives of local towns, villages, and municipalities. It meets every five years to debate and vote on the overall direction of the party. Representatives to the Party Congress vote to confirm the party's choice of president and choose the members of the Central Committee.

The 90-member Central Committee hammers out the details of party policy. It is run by a group of nine department heads responsible for issues similar to those of the government's Council of Ministers. Central Committee members also elect the members of the MPLA's highest body, the Political Bureau. The Political Bureau is made up of 11 members and two alternates. It has a very strong influence on party policy and sets policy when the Central Committee is not convened.

UNITA is the leading opposition party, often arguing in the National Assembly against the dos Santos government's activities and policies. In August 2002, six months after Jonas Savimbi was killed in an ambush, the rebel group officially gave up its armed opposition to the government. UNITA rebels turned over their weapons and participated in an amnesty program sponsored by the government. Since then, UNITA leaders have worked on improving their party's appeal to Angolans. So far their efforts have fallen short, earning them only 16 seats in the 2008 elections (down from 70 in 1992). Isaias Samakuva has led the party since 2003.

Other political parties in Angola include the Social Renewal Party (PRS), which currently holds eight seats in the National Assembly; the National Front for the Liberation of Angola (FNLA), with three Assembly seats; and the New Democracy Electoral Union, which holds two seats.

OIL DRILLING

The petroleum sector is the most important part of Angola's economy, contributing more than half of the country's *gross domestic product (GDP)*. The Angolan government relies on profits from petroleum for 75 percent of its funding.

Currently, Angola's oil industry produces nearly two million barrels of oil a day, and that amount is expected to increase in the next few years. Recent discoveries of new offshore oil fields have almost doubled the estimate of Angola's oil reserves to nearly 20 billion barrels. Angola's most productive oil fields are located under the Atlantic Ocean off the Cabinda coast. If Angola's oil production continues to grow, the country should eventually overcome Nigeria as the largest petroleum producer on the Africa continent.

The state-owned oil company Sociedade Nacional de Combustiveis de Angola (SONANGOL) manages the country's oil resources. SONANGOL usually establishes partnerships with foreign oil companies, selling them drilling rights and a share of the profits. SONANGOL currently has shared ventures with ChevronTexaco, BP, ExxonMobil, Shell, and Canadian Natural Resources, among others.

Most of Angola's oil is exported to foreign countries. The United States and China each buy about 30 percent of Angola's oil. The balance is sold to other countries, notably France, India, South Africa, and Taiwan.

In January 2007, Angola was officially admitted as the twelfth full member of the Organization of Petroleum Exporting Countries (OPEC). OPEC is a cartel that attempts to keep oil a profitable commodity. To do

THE ECONOMY OF ANGOLA

Gross domestic product (GDP*):
$114.1 billion (66th in world)
Inflation: 13.3%
Natural resources: petroleum, diamonds, iron ore, phosphates, copper, feldspar, gold, bauxite, uranium
Agriculture (9.6% of GDP): bananas, sugar cane, coffee, sisal, corn, cotton, manioc (tapioca), tobacco, vegetables, plantains, livestock, forest products, fish
Industry (65.8% of GDP): petroleum; diamonds, iron ore, phosphates, feldspar, bauxite, uranium and gold; basic metal products; fish processing; food processing; brewing; tobacco products; sugar; textiles; ship repair
Services (24.6% of GDP): government, banking, tourism, other

Foreign trade:
Exports–$51.65 billion: crude oil, diamonds, refined petroleum products, coffee, sisal, fish and fish products, timber, cotton
Imports–$18.1 billion: machinery and electrical equipment, vehicles and spare parts, medicines, food, textiles, military goods
Economic growth rate: 5.9%
Currency exchange rate: U.S. $1 = 93.05 Angolan kwanzas (2011)

*GDP is the total value of goods and services produced in a country annually.
All figures are 2010 estimates unless otherwise noted.
Source: CIA World Factbook, 2011.

this, each member country agrees to a production quota. This ensures that the supply of oil will not exceed the demand and helps keep prices stable.

Angola also harvests liquefied petroleum (LP) gas, which can be used for heating, cooking, and to operate vehicles and machinery. The country's LP gas production peaked in 2000 at nearly 1.5 million barrels. However, a new plant to deliver liquefied petroleum gas is scheduled to go online in 2011, which will boost production significantly.

MINING IN ANGOLA

Angola is also known for its mineral resources, particularly diamonds. The Catoca mine in the Lunda Sul province is the world's fourth-largest kimberlite diamond mine. The state-owned diamond firm Endiama produced 9.8 million carats in 2009, worth more thatn $883 million.

Before the civil war Angola was the world's fourth-largest diamond supplier. During the conflict, Angola's diamond territory was mostly under UNITA control, and the rebels used profits from diamond sales to fund their insurrection against the MPLA government. Diamonds used to finance a war are known as *conflict diamonds*, or blood diamonds. In December 2000 the United Nations imposed sanctions on the sale of conflict diamonds because they prolong brutal wars and enable human rights abuses. However, diamond smuggling continues to be a problem in Angola. There is an efficient

Since the end of the civil war, Angola has once again become one of the world's top producers of diamonds.

network of smugglers and it is impossible to guard the miles of river that hold alluvial diamonds.

Although some unauthorized diamonds do get out, the Angolan government and the worldwide diamond industry have tried to battle smugglers by insisting that a certificate of authenticity accompany each gem. This helps ensure that conflict diamonds are not sold to consumers. Although the UN and many national leaders have praised the certification process, it is not foolproof. Smugglers can forge certificates or simply buy official documentation from corrupt bureaucrats.

Another war-related problem that affects Angola's mining industry is the disintegration of the country's infrastructure. It takes a tremendous amount of energy to operate a diamond mine, but Angola's power generation is unreliable. In addition, because many of the country's roads were damaged or destroyed during the war, it is difficult to transport fuel reliably over land. To run the mines, planes loaded with diesel fuel arrive every day.

Diamonds are not Angola's only mineral resource. High-quality iron ore from the Cassinga mine in the Huila region was once an important export. However, production halted during the war and has not yet resumed, although the government recently announced plans to reopen the mine in 2012. Other minerals mined in Angola include phosphates, bauxite (used to make aluminum), uranium, and gold.

AGRICULTURE AND FISHING

Before the civil war Angola had a thriving agricultural sector. The country was the fourth-largest supplier of coffee in the world. The country also produced a great deal of sisal, a strong fiber used for cords and twine. Angola was self-sufficient in food production and exported sugar cane, palm oil, and bananas. However, the UNITA insurgency made farming dangerous, and since it ended in 2002 Angola's agricultural sector has not returned to its prewar levels. Today, less than 3 percent of the land is cultivated, and agriculture provides less than 10 percent of the country's GDP.

A major reason that farming remains dangerous is that Angola has the largest concentration of land mines in the world. According to UNICEF, there are an estimated 10 million land mines buried in Angolan soil. The HALO Trust, an NGO devoted to removing land mines, has identified 289 mine fields in the Huambo province alone. In addition, there is unexploded *ordnance* throughout the countryside. Despite international efforts to remove the land mines, there are plenty of places in Angola where it is unsafe to work or travel.

Nonetheless, the Angolan government is trying to strengthen the agricultural sector. The Ministry of Agriculture is permitting farmers to purchase land and encouraging them to plant such crops as cassava, sugar, beans, millet, palm oil, timber, and tobacco. In addition, the government is taking steps to rehabilitate Angola's coffee industry. New laws have been passed to encourage foreign investment, and several foreign companies have recently formed joint ventures with Angolan coffee plantations.

Rebuilding the coffee industry may be the key to Angola's economic recovery. Because coffee plantations do not require a lot of land, smaller companies can enter the business. This may help stabilize the economy in several areas, whereas if a single company were running large plantations in one

The Angolan port of Namibe is a center for the country's fishing industry.

region, only the people of that area would see the economic benefit.

Rebuilding Angola's fishing industry will also help the country reach its goal of becoming self-sufficient in food production. Angola has nearly 1,000 miles (1,600 km) of coastline, and its waters are rich in mackerel, tuna, and sardines. Before the war, the annual catch of the fishing fleet topped 600,000 tons of fish. It dropped to 35,000 tons during the conflict, but began bouncing back in the late 1990s as Angola began rebuilding its fishing feet with foreign aid. Since the end of the war, fishing has been growing even faster. The government worked with the World Bank to establish the Angolan Support Fund for Fisheries Development, which is intended to help the country's fishermen. One of the organization's projects was to offer training in fishing to 700 people living on the banks of the Zaire River, and supply them with the boats and equipment they needed.

ROADBLOCKS TO ECONOMIC SUCCESS

Three major obstacles hold Angola's economy back. The first is a lack of skilled workers. Before independence, Portuguese Angolans held most of the country's high-skill jobs. When the war broke out, most of these people left for Portugal or other parts of Africa. The sudden disappearance of so many managers and technicians was an immediate blow to the economy. Compounding the problem, the war crippled the national education system, so workers could not be trained to take their places. Consequently, there remains a great need for a sophisticated workforce.

The Capanda Dam is a hydroelectric dam on the Kwanza River in Malanje Province, Angola. The facility, which is 4,600 feet (1,400 m) long and 361 feet (110 m) high generates power by utilizing four turbines. Although construction on the dam began in the 1980s, it could not be completed until after the civil war ended.

Second, the infrastructure of the country—particularly the roads and electrical system—is unreliable. Road transportation remains dangerous because of land mines, and Angola's railroads were damaged during the war. The Benguela Railway runs for 840 miles (1,352 km) across Angola, from the port of Lobito to Luau on the border with the Democratic Republic of the Congo. Currently, only one-third of the track—the 280 miles (451 km) from Lobito to Huambo—can be used. Work is ongoing to complete the line, as well as to rebuild the Luanda Railway. Until transportation and shipping are reliable and safe, commerce will remain difficult and expensive.

During the conflict, UNITA rebels also targeted the country's power grid, and the damage to dams and power lines is still being repaired. Currently, less than 30 percent of the country has access to electricity. Power service is unreliable, with blackouts common even in Luanda. Compounding the problem is that different regions of Angola each have their own separate power grids, which are powered primarily by hydroelectric dams. Angola's government intends to connect the northern, central, and southern systems, but this will be a difficult and expensive project.

Angola's many rivers would be able to generate a lot of electricity if their energy could be properly harnessed. In November 2005 the country finally completed the Capanda Dam, a huge project on the Kwanza River. When it reaches its peak power production, the Capanda Dam will double Angola's electrical generating capacity. Eventually, Angola's leaders hope to link their country's electrical grid to other countries in the region through the South Africa Power Pool (SAPP). Once Angola is tapped into SAPP, it will be able to sell excess power to other countries.

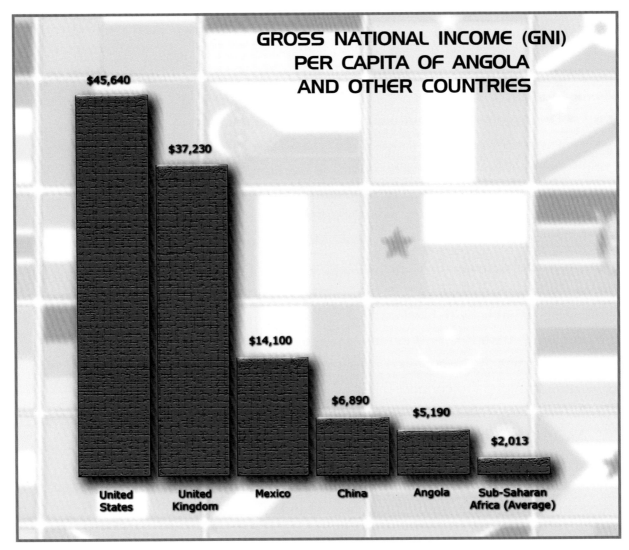

GROSS NATIONAL INCOME (GNI) PER CAPITA OF ANGOLA AND OTHER COUNTRIES

- United States — $45,640
- United Kingdom — $37,230
- Mexico — $14,100
- China — $6,890
- Angola — $5,190
- Sub-Saharan Africa (Average) — $2,013

Gross national income per capita is the total value of all goods and services produced domestically in a year, supplemented by income received from abroad, divided by midyear population. The above figures take into account fluctuations in currency exchange rates and differences in inflation rates across global economies, so that an international dollar has the same purchasing power as a U.S. dollar has in the United States. Source: World Bank, 2011.

Perhaps the biggest threat to Angola's future economic growth is the high level of corruption in the Angolan government. Many officials accept bribes, or use their positions to funnel money and lucrative contracts to themselves and their families. There are 20 Angolans worth more than $100 million, and the top seven have all worked for the government. In 2006, the international watchdog organization Transparency International ranked Angola among the 25 most corrupt countries in the world.

Most of the corruption is related to the oil industry. The specifics of business dealings are kept secret by both the government and the oil companies involved. Human Rights Watch, a ***non-governmental organization (NGO)*** that protects human rights worldwide, estimates that each year some $700 million in bribes, sweetheart deals, and kickbacks is siphoned from the country's oil revenue. That money could have been used to help feed the population or lift people out of poverty.

A change of leadership will not necessarily make the government less corrupt. Unless there are institutions to check the people in power, there will always be the opportunity to abuse the law and misuse government funds. The only way to combat corruption is increased transparency in government and stronger democratic institutions.

Nonetheless, Angola has made progress. Its economy has great potential for growth and the country is attracting greater foreign investment. The future is uncertain, but given Angola's natural resources, the country's economic trend should be upward.

The culture of modern Angola blends African and European elements. (Opposite) An Angolan dancer perform during an festival. (Right) A group of children smile for the photographer on a street near their home in Luanda.

5 The People of Angola

TODAY, ANGOLA IS HOME to approximately 12.8 million people. Historically, most Angolans have lived in rural areas, but since the 1970s the population has drifted toward cities. This trend increased during the civil war, when the Angolan countryside was extremely dangerous. Luanda took the brunt of the displacement, and today about a quarter of the population lives in or around the nation's capital.

Most Angolans—approximately three-quarters of the population—are members of one of three major ethnic groups, the Ovimbundu (37 percent), Mbundu (25 percent), and Bakongo (13 percent). Although there are slight physical differences between each of these groups, the greatest difference is language. Each group speaks a dialect of Bantu that is distinctly different from the others. About 25 percent of the total population are members of other African tribal or ethnic groups.

About 2 percent of Angola's population are *mestiços*—people of mixed African and European descent. Despite their small numbers, Angola's *mestiços* are among the country's most prosperous citizens and play a dominant part in politics. Much of this is due to their education. As the children and grandchildren of Portuguese colonists, *mestiços* had greater access to education and better opportunities for civil service employment. They have passed this advantage on through the generations. A few people of pure Portuguese or European descent also still live in the country.

Many people fled Angola during the civil war. In 2003 the United Nations High Commission on Refugees (UNHCR) began a program to help Angolan refugees. The U.N. transported them back to the country, gave them a supply of food, and provided practical items like farming equipment or tools to build homes. To date, nearly half a million refugees have returned to the country.

RELIGIOUS LIFE

Due to the longstanding influence of Portuguese missionaries, Roman Catholicism is the dominant Western religion in Angola. Beginning in the 1500s Catholic missionaries ventured out among the native Angolans, operating schools and baptizing those who wished to convert. Thirty-eight percent of Angolans are Roman Catholics, while another 15 percent belong to Protestant Christian sects.

As a communist-oriented party, the MPLA was historically opposed to Christianity and other religions, because religions recognize a higher authority (God) than the party itself. During the 1980s, however, the MPLA agreed

Angolan children climb on a ruined tank. Since 2003 the United Nations has been helping Angolan refugees return to their homes.

to allow greater religious freedom. All religious institutions had to register with the government, which then recognized Roman Catholicism and 11 Protestant sects as legal religions. Churches were not allowed to be neutral in the civil war, however. For example, the government banned Jehovah's Witnesses because that faith did not permit military service.

Despite the efforts of missionaries and evangelical Christians, most Angolans still observe traditional beliefs. Africans believe that nature spirits and ancestral spirits have great influence on everyday life. Nature spirits

THE PEOPLE OF ANGOLA

Population: 13,338,541 (July 2011 est.)

Ethnic groups: Ovimbundu, 37%; Mbundu, 25%; Bakongo, 13%; mixed European and native African 2%; European, 1%; other, 22%

Age structure:
0–14 years: 43.2%
15–64 years: 54.1%
65 years and over: 2.7%

Birth rate: 42.91/1,000 population

Infant mortality rate: 175.9 deaths/1,000 live births

Death rate: 23.4 deaths/1,000 people

Life expectancy at birth:
total population: 38.76 years
male: 37.74 years
female: 39.83 years

Population growth rate: 2.034%

Total fertility rate: 5.97 children born/woman

Religions: Indigenous beliefs, 47%; Roman Catholic, 38%; Protestant, 15% (1998 est.)

Languages: Portuguese (official), Bantu and other African languages

Literacy: 67.4% (2001 est.)

All figures are 2011 estimates unless otherwise indicated.
Source: Adapted from CIA World Factbook, 2011.

tend to be associated with location—a tree or a certain gorge, for example. They can also be associated with weather like rain or wind. Ancestral spirits are said to be family members who watch over the affairs of their bloodline. Africans try to honor both types of spirits with rituals, in hopes that the spirits will bring good fortune.

Spirits are not the only sources of magic in the traditional belief system. Some people are said to be able to tap into the magic of the spirit world. Witches and sorcerers use their powers to make others sick or unlucky, while *kimbandas* (diviners), who are said to be able to communicate with the spirits, use their powers to help others and are often familiar with herbal remedies.

These traditional beliefs are taken quite seriously in Angola—even many Christians also ask spirits and *kimbandas* to help them. As recently as 2003, people accused of witchcraft in Angola have been executed for the offense. Some Christian charities make a point of caring for children who have been abandoned because they were thought to be witches.

POVERTY AND HEALTH

Poverty is a major problem in Angola, and approximately 67 percent of the population lives on less than two dollars a day. Many Angolans are malnourished, with some people getting only one meal a day. In rural areas, only 40 percent of all households get their water from a safe source. Even in the cities, many people do not have access to modern sanitation facilities or sources of clean water. Indoor plumbing and electrical service are rare throughout the country. The United Nations recently ranked living conditions in Angola the 11th-worst in the world.

The terrible poverty in Angola makes the country's health situation extremely precarious. Forty-five percent of Angola's children are malnourished, which weakens their immunity to diseases. In areas where the water sources are not clean or sanitation is poor, dangerous bacteria are everywhere. As a result, nearly 17 percent of Angolan children die before their fifth birthday.

The lack of medical facilities compounds the problem. In rural areas, people have to travel many miles on foot just to see a doctor. Often the doctors are

View of a hillside slum near the port city of Lobito. Despite Angola's natural resources, most Angolans are extremely poor.

supplied by a non-governmental organization such as Doctors Without Borders. Many doctors are so busy with critically ill patients that newcomers may have to wait for days. Less severe cases might be turned away completely.

The prevalence of land mines places an enormous strain on Angola's medical system. An unsuspecting traveler who triggers a mine or a child who

landmines remain a major problem in Angola. (Top right) A landmine victim begs on a street in Huambo. (Bottom) A young man marks and deactivates mines in a field near Kuito. Since 2005, more than 50,000 mines have been cleared in Angola, but tens of thousands remain.

picks up a piece of unexploded ordnance might be killed immediately. In many cases, however, that person suffers a debilitating injury, often resulting in the loss of a limb. Angola has more land mines than any other country in the world, and a higher rate of amputees per capita than any other country.

Another health crisis that recently struck Angola was an outbreak of Marburg hemorrhagic fever in the northern part of the Uige province. There is no cure for the Marburg virus, which causes a high fever, diarrhea, vomiting, and severe bleeding. The outbreak killed 227 people between October 2004 and July 2005. Travelers on international flights from Angola were screened in order to keep the virus from spreading. Within the country victims were put in isolation wards where available.

Until relatively recently, Angolans have mostly avoided a health problem that has devastated many

countries in southern Africa: Acquired Immune Deficiency Syndrome, or AIDS. Ironically, the civil war may have helped protect Angolans from the disease, because during the fighting few people—including people already infected with AIDS—visited the country. Since the end of the civil war the number of AIDS cases has risen. Today, it is estimated that more than 2 percent of Angola's population is infected with HIV, the virus that causes AIDS. This seems like a low number when compared to countries like South Africa, where approximately 18 percent of the population has HIV or AIDS. However, the epidemic has already orphaned at least 50,000 Angolan children.

EDUCATION

Like other aspects of Angolan society, the educational system was devastated by the civil war and has not yet recovered. The country has a shortage of trained teachers, and most local governments lack funds for books and other educational materials. Perhaps most importantly, the country does not have enough useable schools. During the war more than 4,000 classrooms were destroyed, and many of the school buildings that remain do not have adequate sanitation or clean water. As a result of these problems, approximately 44 percent of Angolan children did not attend school in 2003, the most recent year for which figures are available.

According to Angolan law, all children between the ages of six and nine are supposed to be enrolled in government-provided primary schools. According to data from UNICEF, only 56 percent of eligible children were enrolled in the four-year primary education program. Of those Angolan children who do attend, more are boys than are girls.

In 2003, the Angolan government announced plans to train 29,000 teachers, with the goal of increasing the percentage of children who attend the free primary schools. So far, that program has helped increase the number of Angolan children enrolled in primary school by 1 million. In addition, UNICEF has helped to fund the construction of many new schools throughout the country.

The country's system of secondary education lasts six to eight years. Of the estimated 2.2 million children of eligible age, only about 400,000 (18 percent) attend secondary school. For those who complete the program of secondary education, Angola has seven universities, including the University of Agostinho Neto and the Catholic University of Angola, which are both located in Luanda.

SPORTS AND RECREATION

Angolans enjoy many sports, but soccer and basketball are among their favorites. Since the late 1980s, Angola's national basketball team has been a dominant force in international competition. Angola has won ten of the last eleven African Men's Basketball Championships, which are held every two years. The country hosted the tournament in 1989, 1999, and 2007. In recent years, Angolan teams have also dominated the African Championship Clubs Cup, a competition of professional basketball clubs.

In soccer, 2006 marked the first year Angola participated in the finals of the World Cup championships. In an emotional match the national team lost to Portugal, one of the best teams in the world, by a respectable 1-0 score. In 2010, Angola further boosted its soccer prominence by hosting the biennial

Angolan soccer fans celebrate their team's qualification for the World Cup tournament in 2006.

Africa Cup of Nations. The team acquitted itself well by winning its group in the opening round, but was ousted in the quarter finals by Ghana. Unfortunately, a terrorist attack on the team from Togo by a separatist group known as the Front for the Liberation of the Enclave of Cabinda marred an otherwise well-organized affair.

Angolans pursue other games as well. Manuel Mateus, for example, was only 17 years old when he earned the rank of international master at chess. He is the youngest African to do so. Angolans also enjoy sailing, team handball, and track and field.

ART AND MUSIC

Angolan art often takes the form of masks. Created from wood, bronze, ivory, or ceramic, masks are an important part of cultural rituals. Some of these rituals occur each year, like the celebration of the harvest. Others mark a change in a person's life, such as passage from childhood to adulthood or from life into death.

Dance is another important part of these rituals. In fact, one of the world's most famous dances may have been based on an Angolan prayer ritual. Samba has its roots in the Angolan word *kuzamba* (to pray). Brazilian plantation owners may have seen slaves actively praying and mistaken it for a dance. Eventually the dance seeped into Brazilian culture.

Perhaps the most famous piece of Angolan art is the Thinker, a Chokwe sculpture of a stylized human figure sitting cross-legged, with its head between its hands. It looks peaceful in its symmetry, as if it is pondering the deep mysteries of life.

Traditional Angolan musical instruments are varied. They include shaking instruments like *saxi* (gourds filled with seeds, similar to maracas) and drums such as *ngoma* (bongos) or *mpwita*, a friction drum with a wooden rod inside. Wind instruments include the *vandumbu*, a soft wooden trumpet, and the *mjemboerose*, made from an antelope horn. Stringed instruments range from the *hungu*, a bowstring that makes music when tapped, to a three-stringed violin called the *kakocha*.

Although Angolans have been telling stories for centuries, their written literature began in 1901 with the publication in Luanda of *Almanach: Essays and Literature*. From there, Angolan literature blossomed, and today includes books of poetry, children's fiction, folk tales, histories, and even detective novels.

One of the best-known contemporary Angolan authors is José Luandino Vieira, whose 1965 short story collection *Luuanda* described life in Angolan shantytowns. In 2006, Vieira won the Camoes Prize, an important literary award in the Portuguese-speaking world.

About one-third of Angola's population lives in cities. (Opposite) The ruins of a church, pockmarked with damage from bullets and shells, in Huambo. Because it was a center for UNITA activity during much of the civil war, Huambo was nearly destroyed by MPLA air strikes in the mid-1990s. (Right) A view of downtown Luanda, the nation's capital.

6 Cities and Communities

MOST ANGOLANS LIVE ON THE BENGUELA PLATEAU in small villages and rural areas. Nonetheless, a sizable percentage—the World Resources Institute estimates around 34 percent—of the population has gravitated toward cities, particularly because of the war. It remains to be seen whether the new urban population will remain, or if it will return to the countryside once the effects of the war subside completely.

LUANDA

The capital city of Angola is Luanda, located on the country's western coast. Luanda is Angola's largest city, with a population estimated at nearly 5 million. The city is home to far more people than it was designed to accommodate. As a result, many parts of Luanda are shantytowns crowded with poor people desperate for work.

Luanda was founded in 1575 by the Portuguese explorer Paulo Dias Novais, and it almost immediately became Angola's busiest seaport. Its main business was in shipping slaves to the Portuguese colonies in Brazil. In 1627 Luanda became Portugal's administrative center in Angola and remained so until Angola's independence in 1975.

Luanda grew at an impressive rate. In 1872 a report by the National Ultramarine Bank called the city "the Paris of Africa" in recognition of its many museums, libraries, concert halls, and other cultural attractions.

Luanda was not built to accommodate the nearly 5 million people who currently live and work there. As a result, shantytowns like this one have sprung up on the outskirts of the city.

Luanda's main industry is oil. There is a sizable refinery in the city, which processes 39,000 barrels a day, despite the damage it sustained during the civil war. Shipping, of course, has always been an important part of the local economy. Recently, a Coca-Cola bottling plant opened just outside the city limits, in Bom Jesus. It has proven so successful that the company has opened a second plant in southern Angola in the city of Lubango. Government officials in Luanda also hope to promote tourism. Several new hotels are planned to cater to travelers eager to see the country now that the war has ended. International travelers arrive and depart from Luanda's Quatro de Fevereiro Airport, the largest airport in Angola.

In addition to being the business center of Angola, Luanda remains the country's cultural center. The city is home to numerous museums, including the Angola Museum and the National Museum of Natural History, as well as more specialized museums such as the Slave Museum, the Coffee Museum, and the Museum of Geology. Luanda also has several libraries, including the National Library of Angola and the National Historical Center.

HUAMBO

Huambo is the capital of the northern Huambo province. It is the second-largest city in Angola, with a population estimated at about 225,000.

Soon after establishing the inland city of Huambo on the high plateau in 1912, the Portuguese renaming it Nova Lisboa (New Lisbon) in 1928. The Portuguese apparently intended to make the city Angola's capital at some future time, but government officials continued to administer the colony from Luanda. In 1975, when Angola became independent, the city's name was changed back to Huambo.

At the time it was an agricultural center and a thriving industrial town, with a fish processing plant, a factory where beer and soda were bottled, and facilities that made goods from leather and plastic. It was also a stronghold for Jonas Savimbi, who established a short-lived alternative government to the MPLA there. During the early 1990s, the MPLA and UNITA fought for control over the town. During this time, much of Huambo was leveled by government air strikes.

With the war over, Huambo is beginning to rebuild. Huambo is now home to a Chinese motorcycle factory that employs many locals. Solar-powered street lights have been installed, and schools and municipal buildings are being rebuilt. The Angolan government has also invested heavily in improving agriculture in the Huambo province, planting approximately a million new coffee plants in 2006 and funding increased production of soybeans, corn, beans, and sweet potatoes. Unfortunately, many fields remain unusable because of land mines.

CABINDA

The Cabinda Province is an Angolan exclave north of the Congo River. Unlike the rest of Angola, the main language spoken in Cabinda is Ibinda, which is derived from the Kikongo language. Currently, Cabinda is home to about 300,000 people. Almost a third of them are refugees from the Democratic Republic of the Congo, which has been torn by civil war and unrest since 1997.

Cabinda produces hardwoods, coffee, rubber, and palm oil, but it's the exclave's substantial reserves of oil that make it so valuable. When the Angolan civil war broke out in 1975, the Front for the Liberation of the Enclave of Cabinda (FLEC) declared Cabinda's independence from Angola. However, the MPLA government, recognizing that Angola would lose most of its revenue if Cabinda became independent, sent an army to squelch the rebellion.

The sentiment for independence has lingered among many residents of Cabinda, but the Angolan army keeps the province under tight control. Human Rights Watch decried the army's practices in a 2004 report, citing examples of unjust detention, torture, and executions without a trial.

BENGUELA

On the coast to the south of Luanda lies Benguela, a city that also serves as capital of the Benguela province. The Portuguese founded the city in 1617. Although Benguela's official population is estimated at between 130,000 and 155,000, no one is certain exactly how many people live in the city. During the civil war, tens of thousands of refugees came to Benguela.

Benguela was once an important port because it was linked to an extensive railroad system, allowing goods to be easily shipped to and from the city. However, the rail lines were destroyed during the civil war, making Benguela less desirable for importers and exporters. The government is currently planning to rebuild a section of the rail line between Benguela and Huambo.

A CALENDAR OF ANGOLAN FESTIVALS

January

On January 1, Angolans celebrate **New Year's Day**. As in the United States, the new year signals the close of Christmas season.

January 4 is **Colonial Repression Martyrs' Day**, commemorating those who suffered under Portuguese rule.

January 8 is **Angolan National Culture Day**. President Agostinho Neto instituted this holiday in 1978.

February

On February 4, the beginning of the armed uprising against the Portuguese colonialists is celebrated as a national holiday.

Carnival is celebrated with a two-day party in the days before Ash Wednesday. (The dates of **Carnival** and **Ash Wednesday** change from year to year; they usually occur in February but can be as late as March 23 in some years.) **Ash Wednesday** is a Roman Catholic holy day that marks the beginning of **Lent**. During the 40-day Lenten season, Angolan Roman Catholics are asked to spend more time reflecting on the life of Jesus Christ.

The final week of Lent is called **Holy Week**, and includes the important Church festivals **Holy Thursday** (commemorating the night of the Last Supper) and **Good Friday** (the day on which Jesus was crucified and died on the cross). Lent ends on **Easter**, the day that Christians observe to remember Jesus' resurrection from the dead. Unlike like the United States and other western countries, Angolans celebrate **Easter** on Monday, as is the custom in Africa.

March

International Woman's Day is a national holiday, celebrated March 8. **Victory Day** is celebrated March 27.

April

The Day of Peace and Reconciliation, April 4, commemorates the signing of the Luena Understanding, the treaty that ended the Angolan civil war.

Youth Day is celebrated on April 14.

May

The first of May is celebrated as **Worker's Day**. As with many other countries, Angola sets aside this day to honor its laborers.

May 25 is **Africa Day**, a holiday to express unity and to celebrate the culture of the continent.

September

On September 17, Angolans celebrate **National Hero Day**, commemorating the birth date of Angola's first president, Dr. Agostinho Neto.

November

Angolans celebrate **Independence Day** on November 11, commemorating the day Portugal relinquished power and Angolans took on self-government.

December

December 25 is **Christmas Day**. Angolans exchange gifts at this time. Even the poorest Angolans try to celebrate the holiday with a better meal than usual. The traditional Angolan Christmas Eve meal is cozido de bacalhau, or cold cooked fish with vegetables. At midnight, people exchange gifts and eat dried fruit. Angolans celebrate with friends and relatives and hold private parties through

New Year's Day.

The government offers a national holiday to coincide with Christmas called **Family Day**.

Corn Funge

2 cups corn flour
4 cups water

Directions:
1. Boil 4 cups water. Slowly add the corn flour. Mix well until you get a consistent paste. Add as much flour as necessary to obtain the consistency.
2. Serve with any fish or meat sauce.

Chicken Muamba

1 chicken
1 large onion, chopped
2 tomatoes, chopped
2 full cups of palm hash (product of the extraction of palm oil)
4 cloves of garlic
17 oz. okra

Directions:
1. Cut the chicken into pieces and season with garlic, salt, black pepper, lemon or vinegar. Add the chopped onion, chopped tomatoes, and the palm hash.
2. Place all but the okra in a pot over medium heat.
3. When the chicken is almost done, add the okra. When the okra is cooked, the muamba is ready to be served. Serve with palm oil beans, funge, or rice.

Cocada Amarela

1 cup sugar
3 cups water
2 whole cloves
1/2 coconut
6 egg yolks
ground cinnamon

Directions:
1. Open the coconut, cut the meat into easy-to-handle pieces, and grate about 2 cups worth.
2. Combine the sugar, water, and cloves in a small saucepan and bring to a boil, stirring constantly. Once it boils, stop stirring and allow it to continue boiling until it reaches the temperature of 230°F (110°C) on a candy thermometer.
3. Reduce the heat to low. With a slotted spoon remove and discard the cloves. Add the grated coconut, a little bit at a time, and mix well. Continue to cook, stirring frequently, for about 10 minutes. The coconut should become translucent. Remove from heat.
4. Beat the egg yolks until they thicken slightly, about 1 minute. Stir in about 1/2 cup of the cooked syrup and mix. Pour this mixture into the saucepan with the remaining syrup and stir together thoroughly.
5. Cook over moderate heat for about 10 minutes, stirring frequently, until the pudding thickens enough to pull away from the bottom and sides of the pan. Spoon the pudding into individual serving plates. Let cool, sprinkle with ground cinnamon and serve.

Palm Oil Beans

2 lb. beans
1 glass palm oil
salt

Directions:

1. Cook the beans until tender. Add the palm oil and salt.
2. Simmer until the oil is cooked. Serve hot.

Camarao Grelhado com Molho Cru (Grilled Prawns with Raw Sauce)

1 lb. prawns

Sauce:
2 cloves garlic, crushed
1/2 cup green onions, including tops, chopped
1 tsp. ground cumin
1/4 tsp. salt
4 tbs. wine vinegar
4 tbs. water

Directions:

1. Make the sauce by combining all the ingredients and grinding them into a paste.
2. Put the prawns on the skewers and brush with sauce. Grill until done (they should lose their translucent color), about 3-4 minutes on each side. Serve with extra sauce on the side.

Frango Grelhado Piri Piri (Grilled Chicken with Peppers)

3 1/2 lbs. chicken parts
2 Tbs. fresh lemon juice
1/4 cup peanut oil
1 finely chopped jalapeño chile or 1/4 tsp. finely minced habañero chile.

Directions:

1. Preheat broiler. Wash the chicken parts and pat them dry. Put chicken pieces in a broiling pan.
2. Mix the lemon juice, peanut oil, and chile together. Brush mixture over the chicken.
3. Place chicken under the broiler and cook until done, about 7-10 minutes on each side. Serve.

Rice Soup

1 lb. stew beef
1/2 lb. beef bones
1 medium onion, minced
1 cup rice
1 tsp. salt
1 bunch mint leaves

Directions:

1. Cut the beef into 1-inch cubes. Wash the bones and place both in a large pot. Add 8 cups water, bring to a boil, then reduce heat to a simmer. Cook until beef is done (approx. 30 minutes).
2. Remove the bones, returning any meat on the bones to the pot. Add onion, salt, rice, and mint.
3. Cover and simmer for 20 minutes. Serves four.

GLOSSARY

alluvial diamonds—diamonds found in the soil of riverbeds, put there by erosion.

arable—land suitable for farming.

assimilado—a native Angolan who adopted Portuguese customs.

Cold War—a worldwide struggle for political, military, and economic dominance involving the United States and the Soviet Union between 1946 and 1991. The superpowers avoided traditional armed warfare by supporting different sides in smaller regional conflicts outside their own countries, such as the civil war in Angola.

Communism—a form of government in which all people are supposed to share equally in the resources of the state. In theory, all of the citizens jointly own all property and businesses; the government, as the peoples' representative, controls all economic activity and distributes to each person their fair share. In practice, communism in Angola resulted in a small group of people who became very wealthy and powerful. This elite used repressive tactics to remain in power.

conflict diamonds—diamonds used to finance a war; also called "blood diamonds."

degredados—Portuguese word for undesirable settlers.

exclave—part of a country that exists outside the borders of the mainland.

gross domestic product (GDP)—the total value of all goods and services produced within a country annually.

indigena—a native Angolan who did not conform to Portuguese behavior.

kimbanda—in the traditional religion of Angola, this was the name for a person who could communicate with the spirit world and heal people.

kimberlite—a type of diamond-rich volcanic rock that occurs in vertical formations known as "pipes."

mestiço—person with a mixed African and European heritage.

non-governmental organization (NGO)—a group that provides aid or social services but is not operated by a particular government.

ordnance—military weapons or supplies, such as ammunition or bombs.

planalto—the high plains of Angola.

pombiero—a Portuguese slave-trading agent.

unicameral—a form of legislature in which all members are part of a single assembly.

PROJECT AND REPORT IDEAS

Visual Project

Many animals left Angola during the civil war. Go to the web site of the Kissama Foundation, www.kissama.org. Research the habitat of the various national parks it lists there. Find pictures of the animals that used to live in Angola's national parks. Then look in encyclopedias to find similar habitats in nearby countries. Put the animal pictures on a poster of a map of Africa, and draw lines to countries with similar habitats where animals could have gone when the war got too close.

Group Discussion

Angola's capital city, Luanda, is overcrowded because people fled the Angolan countryside to escape the fighting. The problem is that the city was not built for the millions of people it now holds. Split up into groups. Imagine that you are the president of Angola, and you want to get the people in Luanda to move back into the countryside. What changes would have to be made? What would you need to build or fix to make the country more appealing? What dangers would you need to remove? Also, what could you do to make the city more livable for the expanded population?

Research Paper

Angola gained its independence from Portugal in 1975. The United States declared its independence from England in 1776. Write a two-page paper comparing the two countries. How were their struggles for independence similar? How were they different? The countries had very different experiences after independence. How was Angola's civil war different from the U.S. Civil War? Are there any ways in which they are alike?

PROJECT AND REPORT IDEAS

Class Presentations

Many non-governmental organizations, such as UNICEF, the HALO Trust, and Doctors Without Borders, have helped the people of Angola a great deal. Find the web site of an NGO that has worked in Angola. Give an oral presentation, answering the following questions: What is the group's mission? What did they do in Angola? Where did they operate in Angola? Where else in the world are they working?

Angola is the country with the highest concentration of land mines in the world. Go to the web sites of some NGOs that deal with land mines, such as the HALO Trust (www.halotrust.org) or the International Committee to Ban Land Mines (www.icbl.org). Give a presentation on the effects of land mines. In what other countries can land mines be found? Why were they put there? How are land mines different from other weapons? What can be done to get rid of land mines once a war is over?

Historical Biographies

Write a one-page biography on one of the following people from Angolan history:

- Agostinho Neto
- Jonas Savimbi
- José Eduardo dos Santos
- Holden Roberto
- Antonio Salazar

CHRONOLOGY

1483: Diogo Cão lands on the coast of present-day Angola and claims the region for Portugal.

1500s: A lucrative slave trade develops in Angola, with most of the slaves being sent to work in the Portuguese colony of Brazil.

1575: The city of Luanda is founded.

1641: The Dutch, allied with some native tribes, invade Angola and capture Luanda. They hold the region until 1648.

1665: Although the Kongo kingdom remains technically independent, it falls under Portuguese influence.

1671: The Portuguese gain control over the Ndongo kingdom.

1836: The Angolan slave trade is outlawed. However, Portugal is unable to enforce the law by itself, and enlists the aid of the British navy.

1858: Slavery is made illegal in Angola.

1884: European countries meet at the Berlin Conference to divide Africa among themselves; the boundaries of Angola are established.

1926: Antonio Salazar comes to power in Portugal; his "New State" policies have a profound effect on life in Angola.

1952: Angolans petition the United Nations for independence. Throughout the decade, the nationalist movement gains support.

1956: The Popular Movement for the Liberation of Angola (MPLA) is formed.

1966: Jonas Savimbi forms the National Union for the Total Independence of Angola (UNITA).

1974: After the Carnation Revolution, Portugal's new leaders agree to independence for Angola.

1975: The MPLA wins a three-way struggle for power. On November 11, the Portuguese relinquish control of the colony.

1979: Agostinho Neto dies and is succeeded by José Eduardo dos Santos.

1988: The Cuban and South African governments agree to withdraw from Angola.

1991: Santos and Savimbi sign the Bicesse Accords on May 31.

1992: Savimbi contests the results of general elections, and UNITA reignites the civil war.

1994: In November, Savimbi signs the Lusaka Protocol.

1997: A unity government involving both dos Santos and Savimbi is established; the United Nations pulls most of its troops out of the country.

1998: The final stage of the civil war begins after UNITA and MPLA leaders disagree on how to govern Angola and the unity government collapses.

2002: Jonas Savimbi is killed by government troops in February. In April, UNITA agrees to a ceasefire and signs the Luena Understanding.

2006: The government postpones elections for the national assembly until 2008.

2007: Angola joins the oil cartel OPEC in January.

2008: First parliamentary elections in 16 years result in a landslide victory for the MPLA.

2009: President dos Santos again delays presidential election; flooding in Cunene leaves 25,000 homeless.

2010: National Assembly ratifies new constitution which abolishes direct election of the president; Angola hosts the African Nations Cup; busload of Togo players attacked by Cabinda separatists.

2012: Angolans hold pro-democracy protests.

Hodges, Tony. *Angola: Anatomy of an Oil State*. Bloomington: Indiana University Press, 2004.

Korff, Granger. *Nineteen With a Bullet: A South African Paratrooper in Angola*. Johannesburg, South Africa: 30 Degrees South, 2009

Meredith, Martin. *The Fate of Africa*. New York: Public Affairs, 2005.

Minter, William. *Apartheid's Contras: An Inquiry into the Roots of War in Angola and Mozambique*. Charleston, S.C.: BookSurge Publishing, 2008

Sheehan, Sean. *Angola*. New York: Marshall Cavendish Children's Books, 2010.

Travel Information

http://www.lonelyplanet.com/angola
http://travel.state.gov/travel/cis_pa_tw/cis/cis_1096.html
http://www.world66.com/africa/angola

History and Geography

http://lcweb2.loc.gov/frd/cs/aotoc.html
http://geography.about.com/library/cia/blcangola.htm
http://www.factmonster.com/ipka/A0107280.html

Economic and Political Information

http://www.angola.org.uk/Default.aspx?IDM=4&IDLang=1
http://news.bbc.co.uk/2/hi/africa/country_profiles/1063073.stm
http://angola.usembassy.gov/

Culture and Festivals

http://www.angola.org/culture.html
http://www.paulahollinsdesigns.com/pages/MbiraLinks/MbiraAngolaLinks.html
http://www.everyculture.com/A-Bo/Angola.html

The Embassy of The Republic of Angola
2100-2108 16th Street, NW
Washington, DC 20009
Tel: (202) 452-1042
Fax: (202) 452-1043
Website: http://www.angola.org

U.S. Embassy in Luanda, Angola
Rua Houari Boumedienne #32
Luanda, Angola
Tel: (+244) 222-641-000
Fax: (+244) 222-641-259
Website: http://luanda.usembassy.gov

Permanent Mission of the Republic of Angola to the United Nations
820 Second Avenue, 12th Floor,
New York, NY 10017
Tel: (212) 861-5656
Fax: (212) 861-9295
Website: http://www.un.int/wcm/content/site/angola

Publisher's Note: The websites listed on these page were active at the time of publication. The publisher is not responsible for websites that have changed their address or discontinued operation since the date of publication. The publisher reviews and updates the websites each time the book is reprinted.

INDEX

African traditional religions, 59–61
agriculture, 15, 47, 50–51
   See also economy
AIDS/HIV, 62–63
   See also health care
Almanach: Essays and Literature, 66–67
Angola
   area, 13, 15
   borders, 11–12, 13
   cities, 69–73
   civil war, 27–31
   climate, 13–15
   culture, 57–67
   ecological challenges facing,
      16–17
   economy, 45–51
   education, 63–64
   geographic features, 11–12, 15
   government, 35–43
   history, 19–33
   independence, 25–27
   provinces, 36
   wildlife, 16–17
area, land, 13, 15
art, 66–67

Bakongo people, 19–20, 57
   See also history
Benguela, 22, 73
Benguela Railway, 52
Berlin Conference, 23–24
Bicesse Accords, 31
   See also civil war
borders, 11–12, 13

Cabinda (exclave), 12, 23, 72–73
Caetano, Marcello, 27

Cão, Diogo, 20
Capanda Dam, 53
Carnation Revolution, 27
   See also history
cities
   Benguela, 22, 73
   Cabinda (exclave), 12, 23, 72–73
   Huambo, 14, 32, *69*, 71–72
   Luanda, 12, 14, 22, 27, 57, 69
   Namibe, 14
civil war, 27–33, 73
   and conflict diamonds, 48–49
climate, 13–15
conflict diamonds, 48–49
   See also diamonds
Congo River, 12
constitution, 35–36, 38
   See also government
corruption, government, 53, 55
Costa, Adalberto, 39
Council of Ministers, 38
   See also government
Council of the Republic, 39–40
   See also government
Cuanza River, 12
Cubango River, 12
Cuito Cuanavale, 31
culture
   art and music, 66–67
   education, 63–64
   ethnic groups, 57–58, 60
   health care, 61–63
   religions, 58–61
   sports and recreation, 64–65
Cunene River, 12, *14*

da Costa, Desiderio, *48*

de Miranda, Joao Bernardo, *40*
diamonds, 11, 15–16, 17, 45, 48–49,
   51
dos Santos, Fernando da Piedade
   Dias, 36–37
dos Santos, José Eduardo, 30–32, *35*,
   36, 38

ecological challenges, 16–17
economy, 45, 54, 71
   agriculture, 15, 47, 50–51
   fishing industry, 51
   and government corruption, 53,
      55
   and infrastructure, 52–53
   mining industry, 48–49, *51*
   oil, 45–47, 71, 73
education, 63–64
Epupa Falls, *11*
ethnic groups, 57–58, 60

geographic features, 11–12, 15
   and ecological challenges, 16–17
government, 35–36, 42–43
   corruption, 53, 55
   executive branch, 36–39
   judicial branch, 41–42
   legislative branch, 39–40
   See also political parties
Great Britain, 23
gross domestic product (GDP), 46, 47
   See also economy
gross national income (GNI), 54
   See also economy

health care, 61–63
history

Numbers in **bold italic** refer to captions.

Bakongo people, 19–20
Bushmen, 19
civil war, 27–33, 73
independence, 25–27
under Portugal, 22–27
and the slave trade, 20–23, 70
Holland, 22–23
Huambo, 14, 32, *69*, 71–72
Human Rights Watch, 55
"hut tax," 23

independence, 25–27
infrastructure, *45*, 49, 52–53

Kongo kingdom, 20–22, 23
See also history

land mines, 15, *19*, 50, 62
languages, 60, 72
literacy rate, 60
Luanda, 12, 14, 22, 27, 57, 69–71
Luanda Railway, 52
Luena Understanding, 33
Lusaka Protocol, 32

Maieco, Fabrice Alcebiade, 65
Massangano, 22
Mateus, Manuel, 65
Mbundu ethnic group, 57
mestiços, 23, 24–25, 26, 58
See also ethnic groups
mining industry, 48–49, *51*
music, 66–67

Namibe, 14
National Assembly, 36–37, 38, 39
See also government

National Front for the Liberation of
Angola (FNLA), 25, 27–29, 43
See also National Union for the
Total Independence of
Angola (UNITA)
National Union for the Total
Independence of Angola
(UNITA), 27–29, 31–33, 42–43,
48–49
natural resources, 11, 15–16, 17,
45–49
Ndongo kingdom, 20–22
See also history
Neto, Agostinho, 25, 27, *28*, 29–30
Nova Lisboa (New Lisbon). *See*
Huambo
Novais, Paulo Dias, 70

oil, 45–47, 71, 73
Okavango River, 12
Organization of Petroleum
Exporting Countries (OPEC),
46–47
Ovimbundu ethnic group, 57

political parties, 25, 27–33, 35, 38–39,
42–43
See also government
Popular Movement for the
Liberation of Angola (MPLA),
25, 27–33, 42, 58–59
population, 57, 60
Portugal, 20–27

Quicama National Park, 17

refugees, 58, *59*, 72–73

religions, 58–61
republic government. *See* government
Roberto, Holden, 25, 27, *29*

Salazar, Antonio, 24, 26–27
Samakuva, Isaias, 43
Savimbi, Jonas, *19*, 27, 29, *30*, 31–33,
38, 43, 72
Serra da Chela mountains, *11*, 12
Silva, Anibal Cavaco, *37*
slave trade, 20–23, 70
Sociedade Nacional de
Combustiveis de Angola
(SONANGOL), 46, *48*
See also oil
South Africa Power Pool (SAPP), 53
Soviet Union, *28*, 29–31
Spinola, Antonio de, 27
sports and recreation, 64–65
Supreme Court (Tribunal da
Relação), 39–40, 41

tourism, 71
Transparency International, 55

United Nations, 25, 31, 32–33
United States, 25, 29–31, 46

Vicente, Manuel, *48*
Vieira, José Luandino, 67

wildlife, 16–17
World War II, 25

CONTRIBUTORS/PICTURE CREDITS

Professor Robert I. Rotberg is Director of the Program on Intrastate Conflict and Conflict Resolution at the Kennedy School, Harvard University, and President of the World Peace Foundation. He is the author of a number of books and articles on Africa, including *A Political History of Tropical Africa* and *Ending Autocracy, Enabling Democracy: The Tribulations of Southern Africa.*

Rob Staeger lives and writes in New Jersey. He is the author of numerous books and stories for young readers, including *The Boom Towns*, *Native American Sports and Games*, and *Asylees* for Mason Crest Publishers. He has also written several plays for older audiences.